Cream Puff Days

and
CHOCOLATE FUDGE
NIGHTS

Enjoy ♥ Karen Crum

Cream Puff Days
and
CHOCOLATE FUDGE
NIGHTS

Copyright © 2019 by Karen Linton Crum
Published by: Mitera Press • Louisville, Kentucky

Written by Karen Linton Crum • illustrations by Bill Brown
ISBN: 9780998078229
Library of Congress Number: 2018907040

—————— Summary ——————

It's a cream puff kind of day. So begins this tender story of a mother and her young daughter
as they bake treats together—treats filled with love. The rhythmic text and sweet words will
draw you in and take hold. Parent and child will read this again and again. There are two recipes
included: Cream Puffs and Chocolate Fudge, both special recipes handed down by the author's
mother. *Cream Puff Days and Chocolate Fudge Nights* reminds all of us of those precious times
we spend together in the kitchen. Time spent together is the sweetest gift of all.

LOUISVILLE, KY
MITERA PRESS
U.S.A.

To
Regina A. Linton,
a loving mother and
wonderful baker

"It's a cream puff kind of day," Mama said,
her eyes bright as she pulled on her apron
and tied the strings tight.

1

I jumped up and down   as I heard
the rain fall, because cream puff days were
the best days of all!

The old worn oven came alive
and began to glow.

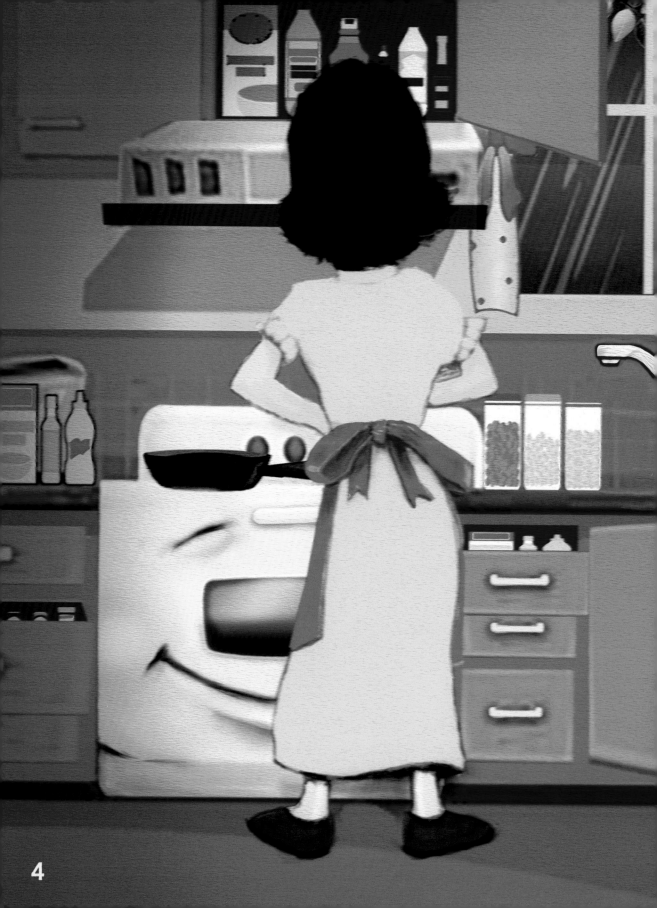

As Mama gathered ingredients
from cabinets high and low.

First, she put water, butter, and salt in
the pan until the bubbles began to rise.

Then, Mama showed me how to add flour
and stir until a ball formed before my eyes.

Mama moved the pan off the heat for just a short time. We added the eggs and whipped to a shine.

We carefully dropped the
puffs on a sheet to bake.

My tummy growled.

How much longer can they
possibly take?

The puffs were cooled and filled with sweet cream. After all that waiting, it felt like a dream.

Watching the rain with a cream puff
to share; there was nothing else that
could ever compare!

On cold, snowy nights, Mama would say with a wink, "It feels like a chocolate fudge kind of night, don't you think?"

14

I danced all around   as the snow
piled up tall, because chocolate fudge
nights were the best nights of all!

We melted milk, sugar, syrup and
chocolate over a low heat.

16

Then added butter and vanilla,
and started to beat.

We stirred until our arms were tired
and the mixture was thick.

Then Mama buttered the pan so
the fudge would not stick.

The fudge was chilled and
cut in small squares.

Mama poured us some milk,
while I pulled up our chairs.

21

Darkness fell,
with the snow coming down.

We shared more fudge
without making a sound.

I know that those times with
Mama and me were sweeter than
a cream puff or fudge
could ever be.

25

Recipes

CREAM PUFFS

Ingredients:
1 cup water
½ cup butter or shortening
1 teaspoon salt
1 cup flour
4 pasteurized eggs

Add butter to water and bring to a boil. Add flour all at once and stir until a ball forms in the center of the pan. Remove from heat and add eggs one at a time, beating after adding each egg. Drop by the spoonful on a cookie sheet and bake 15 minutes in a 450 degree oven. Reduce heat to 350 degrees and continue to bake for an additional 30 minutes. Cool and fill with ice cream, whipped cream or cream filling (see below).

CREAM FILLING

Ingredients:
1/3 cup flour
2/3 cup sugar
¼ teaspoon salt
2 cups milk
3 tablespoons butter
3 pasteurized egg yolks, beaten
1/2 teaspoon vanilla

Mix flour, sugar, and salt. Boil milk and add to dry mixture slowly and continue to stir. Cook over hot water, stirring until thick. Add butter and pour mixture over egg yolks, stirring constantly. Cool then add vanilla, stir, and mixture is ready.

CHOCOLATE FUDGE

Ingredients:
2 cups sugar
2/3 cup milk
2 tablespoons corn syrup
3 ounces unsweetened chocolate
2 tablespoons butter
1 teaspoon vanilla

Put sugar, milk, syrup and chocolate in a saucepan and stir until the sugar is dissolved. Cook slowly over a low heat, then add butter and vanilla and beat until the mixture is thick. Pour into a greased pan and chill. Cut into small squares when firm.

About Karen Linton Crum

Karen Linton Crum grew up with a love of reading and baking with her mother. A graduate of Western Kentucky University, she worked in sales and marketing, but always dreamed of writing children's books. After raising three children, Karen has penned her first children's book, *Cream Puff Days and Chocolate Fudge Nights*, as a tribute to her mother and a legacy for future generations.

Stay Connected with Karen at:
www.klcrum.com

About Bill Brown

At age 5, Bill drew outlines of characters for his kindergarten classmates to color. Later, he helped finance his studies at Western Kentucky University by doing caricatures at an amusement park, which led to becoming an editorial cartoonist for the college newspaper. He has been illustrating and designing ever since his college days. Bill's hobbies include music, sports, and film.

Cream Puff Days
and
CHOCOLATE FUDGE
NIGHTS